NORTH DAKOTA NEVER GIVE UP

Guide to front cover photographs

John Hancock	Roger Maris	Clara Aasen
Fritz Pollard	Angie Dickinson	John C. West
Lynn W. Aas	Eric Sevareid	Frank Eversull
Peggy Lee	Lawrence Welk	Milton Aasen

LARRY AASEN

Copyright © 2019 by Larry Aasen
ISBN **978-0-578-48791-5**

Published in the United States of America
By Ellery Press, a division of Publicity Ink
31 Ellery Lane
Westport, CT 06880
Printed in Fargo, North Dakota

Any part of this book may be used or reproduced in any manner *without* permission from the author.

For all general information, or to order additional copies, contact Ellery Press at:
Telephone: **(207) 466-9274**
E-mail: **ElleryPress@gmail.com**

Also by Larry Aasen
North Dakota Tales (1990)
My Friend the Pig (1994)
More North Dakota Tales (1996)
Salute to North Dakota Writers (1998)
North Dakota Postcards (Arcadia Publishing, 1999)
North Dakota Images (Arcadia Publishing, 2000)
North Dakota 100 Years Ago (Ellery Press, 2009)

Contents

Introduction v
1. Farming 1
2. Clara's Diary 18
3. A Norwegian Bachelor Farmer 24
4. Going To School 29
5. Farm Kids 33
6. Weather 38
7. Family Size 41
8. Going to NDAC (1941-1943) 47
9. Going to UND in the 1940's 53
10. World War II 61
11. Cars 70
12. Christmas 73
13. They Never Gave Up 76
About the Author 82

Acknowledgements

The people and publications below were extremely helpful in providing photos and historical items for this book.

Martha Aasen
Susan Aasen
Barbara Engel Beebe
Annie Bennett, *North Dakota Horizons*
John Hallberg, NDSU Archives
Leif Jonasson, *The Spectrum of NDSU*
Bob Lind, *The Forum of Fargo-Moorhead*
Hillsboro Banner
NDSU
UND
Tom and Cay Pierce
Allan and Ona Ellenson
North Dakota Historical Society
John Kolness, Heritage Press
Grand Forks Herald
Ted Horowitz
Sarah M. Walker, North Dakota State Archives

David Rutkin put this book together and he did good. Very good. He also did my last book. He is an expert and we thank him very much.

INTRODUCTION

North Dakotans never give up.

That sounds like I am writing an advertisement for North Dakota.

North Dakota doesn't need that. As I am 96 years old, I have watched, known or read about a lot of North Dakotans who did not give up.

I will tell you about a few of them in this book.

Peggy Lee was seventh of eight children in a very poor family. Her dream was to be a famous singer. She headed for Hollywood at the age of 17! She made it.

Lawrence Welk was sixth of eight children living on a small farm in North Dakota. He quit school in the fourth grade (it may not have been his decision) to help his Dad. He promised to stay with his Dad until he was 21. He did and then he bought an accordion on credit—and the rest is history. People laughed at his music for years — and Welk laughed at them — as he headed for his bank.

A farm widow in North Dakota had to manage the farm after her husband was killed in a car accident, leaving her with three little kids. Then she found out her renter was cheating her. He thought he could get away with it. He could not.

This book also is a "memoir" because gives a picture of life and times in the 1940's in North Dakota. We hope that young people — and adults — will be encouraged to never give up.

Most of all I hope it makes my fellow North Dakotans proud, again and again, of North Dakota — the state that never gives up.

— *Larry Aasen*

One
FARMING

In 1924, the entire Ole Aasen family gathered for a picnic at the Ole Aasen farm near Perley, Minn., near the North Dakota border. The author is in the front row (white shirt), second from the left.

North Dakota pioneers came to this country for farmland of their own, to cultivate out of the wilderness. In the 1870's there was very little opportunity in Norway, home to so many of our forebears. The farms there were small, rocky and often located on hillsides. My grandfather, Ole Aasen, was a typical Norwegian immigrant.

Ole Aasen learned that in America he could get free land, if he lived on it for five years and fulfilled all the requirements of the Homestead Act of 1862, signed into law by Abraham Lincoln. He was able to get passage on a ship and arrived at Ellis Island in New York in 1870 at age 25. A train took him to Minnesota and by the time he reached Fargo, N.D., he had just seven dollars in his pocket to begin his new life.

> **FREE HOMES IN DAKOTA**
> **21,000000 ACRES OF VACANT GOVERNMENT LAND**
> **OPEN TO SETTLERS**
> **UNDER THE HOMESTEAD PRE-EMPTION AND TIMBER CULTURE LAWS**
> **OFFICIAL MAPS AND FULL INFORMATION ABOUT EVERY PART OF**
> **NORTH AND SOUTH DAKOTA**
> **IN REGARD TO SOIL, CLIMATE, PRODUCTS ADVANTAGES AND DEVELOPMENT – AGRICULTURE, MANUFACTING COMMERCIAL AND MINERAL-THE GOVERNMENT LAND LAWS ETC.**
> **FURNISHED CHERRFULLY AND FREE ON APPLICATION TO**
> **F.H. HAGERTY**
> **COMMISIONER OF IMMIGRATION**
> **ABERDEEN, DAKOA**

Ads like this ran in Norway to recruit settlers. They were printed in Norwegian and English.

But like the other settlers in that great wave from Scandinavia, Ole Aasen would not, and indeed, could not, give up. For many years Norwegians were the largest group of new Americans in North Dakota.

Ole homesteaded on a tract of 80 acres near Perley, Minn., in the Red River Valley. It's hard to believe, but records indicate some settlers actually lived in caves before they were able to build sod houses. Family legend has it this is how Ole spent the early days on his land. To make money so he could start farming, he worked as a hired hand for other farmers and for a blacksmith, shoeing horses.

He planted wheat, and he knew how to farm it. He also made money selling "stove lumber" from the trees on his land, and sold everything from calves and cream to the skins of skunks. Land was cheap, and he kept buying a little more each year. In 1881, he married another Norwegian immigrant, Mary Lein, a "petite little lady, hardly weighing 100 pounds." Yet, Mary could drive five horses by herself, and often rowed herself across the Red River. Ole and Mary were by then living in style — in a one-room log house.

When Ole died in 1925, that seven dollars had grown to an estate of $18,667, but more importantly, he gave each of his six children 80 acres of land. The next generation would see a revolution in the farming that had given them life in the United States.

In the 1930's, we knew drastic changes in North Dakota farming were coming when our farm went from eight horses to two, and a new John Deere tractor, painted green, stood in our yard. My uncle would not tell me what happened to the other six horses. We kept two to clean out the barn and assist in other farm jobs, like haying.

Haying time in July was hot, hard work, but necessary if the cows were going to eat that winter. The grass would be cut, raked into piles, picked up by men in a wagon (called a hayrack), and taken to the barn. Then, a thick rope would pull a sling holding the hay up into the hayloft (while everyone yelled, "There she goes!").

The change from horse farming to tractor farming had many implications, most of them good. The land needed to produce hay and oats for the horses could now be used for cash crops. Tractors could — and often were — run all night if necessary, whereas the horses were worn out at sunset and returned to the

Harvest operation

barn. The downside? You could grow what the horses needed to eat, but had to pay cash for gasoline, and that cost more than the horses.

My uncle, Alfred Brenden, eventually bought a large tractor. It was expensive but it gave him a lot of comforts as he worked the fields; he could watch TV, listen to the radio and eat his lunch in a little room called a cab without being bothered by flies or dust.

In the 1940's many small farmers began to sell their land and move into town. The big landowners snapped up the small farms as soon as they could. Much changed on our farm at this time. About 10 to 15 hired men were no longer needed. Fewer farmers continued to raise cows, pigs, chickens or turkeys.

New insecticides and fungicides have given farm products more protection from disease and insects. And now, farmers have gone

The hardest part about haying in July was watching the city folks drive by in their white shirts, on their way to the cool Minnesota lakes. That may be what I was seeing here one hot afternoon, on a haying break with my friend Mervin Eidum.

from using horses to survey and till their fields, to using flying drones to measure, inspect, spray and photograph the crops.

North Dakota farmers have never stopped innovating and have never given up. Yet the single biggest threat to farming over the years is ever constant: the unpredictable North Dakota weather!

Traditional threshing before the arrival of the combine.
Fred Hultstrand History in Pictures Collection, NDIRS-NDSU, Fargo.

One farmer who never gave up was my brother, Milton. He was a very strong man who easily shoveled grain and handled everything on the farm. But slowly he was stricken with multiple sclerosis (MS), and his legs no longer worked. Milton couldn't bear to sit still, so he bought an airplane and taught himself to fly — rigging up all the controls on the steering wheel where he could easily reach them. He became the President of the North Dakota Flying Farmers Association.

During the Great Depression and drought of the 1930's, grasshoppers threatened crops. When the crops were entirely eaten up, the grasshoppers ate clothes hanging on clotheslines, the straw off brooms, and even gnawed on fence posts.

State Historical Society of North Dakota

Farm women did not give up. When this woman lost her husband in a car accident, she not only continued to do the housework and raise the kids, but she fed the pigs and chickens and did many other farm jobs. When a renter thought he could cheat her, he found that he could not. She never gave up!

The Aasen barn, Hillsboro, North Dakota

Our old barn deserves a few words because it played a big part in our lives in the 1930's and early 1940's.

First of all our barn had prestige when it was built in 1913 because it was larger than most around and farmers were often judged by the size of their barn.

For we three Aasen boys, it was a place to hide, to play, to fight, to swing on the hay ropes and to practice trapeze acts.

We all spent a lot of time cleaning the barn, milking the cows (and I HATED milking the cows), turning the cream separator and teaching the calves how to drink. To teach a calf how to drink, we would put our fist in the bottom of a full pail of milk and then let the calf suck one finger. It was a strange sensation, a wet and messy procedure—but it worked. All our calves learned to drink! Now I wonder how the buffalo calves learned to drink?

We timed out milking sessions so we wouldn't miss out favorite radio programs like Fibber McGee and Molly, and Amos and Andy.

Barbara Engel Beebe
Taft Grain Elevator
Gouache on paper, 17" x 14"
©1996
JonathanFrostGallery.com

This grain elevator in Traill County, ND, no longer exists. It was made of wood; today most elevators are made of steel or concrete. The painting was created by Barbara Engel Beebe who hauled grain here in the 1940's when she was growing up on her family's farm in nearby Cummings. She has also painted the St. Olaf Lutheran Church in Traill County. She now lives on a small island off the coast of Maine, where she has no electricity or running water. But she never gave up her dream to be an artist.

In the late 1930's, large cumbersome combines appeared in North Dakota. It was a startling development, and meant many farm hands would be out of work. Only a few people were necessary to run the combine, while it took 20 to 30 men to harvest and thresh grain. The workers resented the machines, and there were rumors of rock throwing and sabotage.

Had he lived to see them, Milton Aasen, the flying farmer, would have been tickled and intrigued by these drones and would have been among the early experimenters. Photo: Kinwun.

Speaking of sunflowers, North Dakota and South Dakota lead the nation in production of sunflowers. North Dakota farmers produced around 740 million pounds in 2018.

And North Dakota leads the U.S. in production of spring wheat, durum wheat, dry edible peas, dry edible beans, honey, flaxseed and canola.

39.1 million acres — nearly 90% of North Dakota's land area — is in farms and ranches.

Mexican Bracero farm workers weeded, thinned and harvested sugar beets during World War II.
Institute for Regional Studies, NDSU, Fargo.

During World War II, as young men left farms to go to war, many farmers looked for other sources of labor.

The Bracero Program was a series of laws and diplomatic agreements, initiated in August 1942, that allowed Mexican farm workers to enter the United States as guest workers during the growing season. ("Bracero" is a Spanish word that means "laborer.") The agreement guaranteed decent living conditions (sanitation, adequate shelter and food) and a minimum wage of 30 cents an hour or $3 per day living allowance if they were unemployed on rainy days or when harvest ended. Housing and sanitation facilities had to meet certain standards. The program also allowed the importation of contract laborers from Guam during the early phases of the war.

Our farm hired about 15 Mexicans every summer. They would send their earnings back to Mexico by Western Union. On Sunday, some of the kids would be taken (dragged) to a local church. The kids did not understand the words but they liked the singing and organ music.

The Hired Men

1941

Aasen's mother took this photo with a $1 box camera. For personal reasons, one of the men did not want to show his face.

By Larry Aasen

The men jumped off freight trains at Taft, North Dakota, four miles north of Hillsboro, North Dakota. They had been riding in train box cars and looked like it. They wore dirty, ragged overalls. Riding in a railroad box car for many miles did not help their appearance. A few of the men were lucky and came in beat-up, old cars.

They were not bums. Most of them had left farms in Minnesota, Iowa, South Dakota, and other neighboring states. Some had owned farms that failed. Others could not find jobs anyplace because of the severe Depression in the 30's and 40's. We kids would wave at the men riding the trains and they would wave back. We thought we were cheering them up!

They walked about a half a mile to the Alfred Brenden farm where I lived with my mother, grandmother and two brothers. We were under 10 years of age and curious — and a little afraid — of these men coming to our farm. My mother and grandmother were not surprised by the visit. It happened a lot during the Depression.

The ladies went to work at once and handed out as much food as they could find in the house. I can't remember what they got for food but I am sure it was not very fancy. I do remember the ever-present red or green jello. We three kids just stared at the men.

This article originally appeared in North Dakota Horizons (Fall 2018).

John Duka, an immigrant from Armenia, worked on our farm every year. Standing next to him and the log cabin where they were born, are, left to right, Milton, Lawrence and Tilford Aasen.

They didn't even see us because they were busy gulping their food. We had never seen so many uninvited men on our farm. The men were quiet, polite, and not laughing or making jokes. They had been beat up by the Depression and it showed. And they were not used to begging for food.

After eating they talked to Alfred Brenden, my uncle who farmed the land. Alfred, a tall, gruff, thin bachelor who rolled his own cigarettes, worked hard six days a week all his life. He farmed with eight horses as well as with tractors. For some reason, he never owned a rain coat. Like all farmers, I think he was just so happy when it rained that he didn't mind getting wet.

Alfred was the boss and you didn't forget it. Yet he was fair, honest and respected by other farmers. As my Dad was killed in a car accident when I was five years old, Alfred was my surrogate father and he was an excellent surrogate.

The men would tell Alfred they were looking for a job, any kind of work. Before hiring anybody, Alfred would always look at the palms of their hands to see if they showed signs of hard work. He didn't need resumes.

The men who were not hired walked slowly back to Taft to catch the next train—if it stopped.

Today, the back breaking work they did would be called "intensive." They picked up bundles of grain and made small stacks with about eight bundles. A wagon pulled by two horses would take the grain bundles to the threshing machine. The men would toss the grain bundles into the threshing machine. Grain would go into a waiting truck and straw would blow out a big pipe at the end of the machine.

The grain would be put in trucks and taken to Taft to sell—an anxious moment because the grain might be less than top quality.

Long days were spent working in the hot sun, fighting flies and mosquitos and sometimes, a dust storm.

The men got a dollar a day. The men who had special jobs got $1.25. Alfred set the hourly wage. There were few labor unions at that time.

1940

On Sundays, the men would go to a gravel pit near Cummings to swim.

The men slept on hay in the barn. When they left the barn at the end of the harvest season, we kids would dig through the hay to look for anything we could find. We would uncover lurid sex and crime magazines, cigarettes, dirty socks, underwear, and other very personal items we had never seen before. One time when I was moving the hay with a pitch fork, I accidently ran it through a gallon tin can containing alcohol. I was told that one man got tears in his eyes as the alcohol dribbled to the floor. The men ignored me and Alfred never let us go into the hay loft again. The drink of the day was hot water with sugar and alcohol. Alfred never drank because he wanted to be in charge at all times. For many years we always thought he would marry our hired girl—but he never did.

To feed some 15 men at a long table, two tables were pushed together. My mother said that nearly all of the men had two helpings and some three.

As there were no showers on the farm, we suspected that some men took baths in the big, round water tanks for the cattle and horses. On Sunday all the men would go up to a gravel pit near Cummings, N.D., to swim (and take a bath). Some of the men even had swimming suits.

These five men are going to work in the field. They are not smiling.

The Hillsboro, N.D., Banner never reported any news stories about these men breaking any laws. For many years we had about 15 hired men and they became our friends. Some came back again and again.

Only Alfred knew the last names of the men because he wrote the checks. They had nick-names like Swede, Red, or Ole. One was called "Skinny Bone Tight" and we never knew why.

Sometimes at night one of the men would play his guitar and some would sing. For us kids, this was the high point of the day!

When the harvest was over, the men would go back to Taft and catch a train. They didn't know where they would end up but it did not make much difference.

Three hired men, two kids and the ever-present dog rest after lunch.

Two

CLARA'S DIARY

My mother Clara Brenden Aasen was a farm widow with three kids who lived near Fargo, N.D, in a log house without electricity, running water or central heating. After her husband was killed in a car accident, Clara ran the farm.

She kept a diary from 1916 to 1953. Here are some samples from her 30 diaries that are a view of North Dakota history at that time—and a look at her very tough life as a woman farmer, a mother, and a businesswoman.

She seldom used adjectives or adverbs and wasted few words in her diary. More important than what she said was often what she left unsaid. Many of her diary comments are more like headlines than paragraphs. For example, on July 27, 1935, she said simply, "Rust has destroyed this year's wheat crop."

April 12, 1918: My brother Oliver Brenden left from Camp Dodge, Iowa for somewhere in France.

March 22, 1919: Butchered two pigs today. Gave neighbor half of one pig.

December 5, 1922: Lawrence Obert Aasen is born. Because of a bad snow storm, Dr. Gowenlock arrived too late. His car got stuck and he finally got here with a team of horses. Three ladies were here to help me.

May 20, 1923: Today we saw our first airplane fly right over our log house.

May 21, 1927: Captain Charles Lindberg *[sic]* flew his famous airplane "Spirit of St. Louis" 3600 miles in 33 hours.

Oliver Brenden leaves his home farm in Eldorado Township, N.D. in 1917 to return to Camp Dodge, Iowa, and then to leave for World War I in France. One of his duties was to be company bugler. He died in 1922 as a result of poison gas used by the Germans.

June 23, 1928: Such a day. Theodore, my husband, died from a car accident.

October 25, 1928: I have now done all the farm work for 4 full days.

February 6, 1930: Carl Ben Eielson, Arctic flyer from Hatton, N.D. crashed January 25 and he was buried on March 26, 1939.

December 31, 1930: Charles Bannon, who killed 6 people in North Dakota, was hanged by a mob of 60 people who overpowered the sheriff.

January 16, 1932: Rev. A.J. Tjornhom spoke on sin today in church.

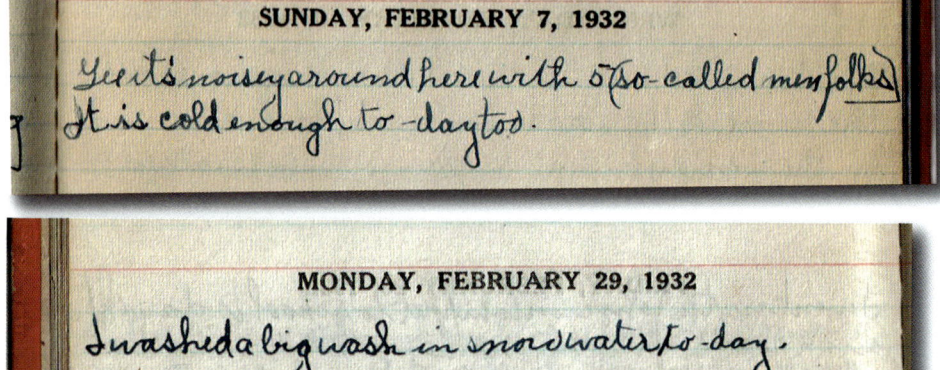

March 2, 1932: The Charles Lindberg [sic] baby was kidnapped from his crib in Hopewell, N.J. last night. I was over to George's today. Took over 3 blouses that I had sewed. 1 pair pillowcases and fitted a pink dress for Violet with bloomers.

April 12, 1932: People's State Bank in Hillsboro closed today. Tonight the whole town is in a terrible stir over the bank.

TUESDAY, MAY 24, 1932

Washed to-day. In May 1932 Mrs Em Earhart (Putnam) lady flier crossed the ocean in less then 15 hours, she worked her own way up working for a telephone Co. saved her money took flying lessons and "broke records and achieved fame.

Monday ~~SUNDAY~~, SEPTEMBER 4, 1932 *Labor Day.*

Oh yes a real labor day. I done a big clothes washing. Miss Florence Klingensmith aged 26 years. North Dakota's only lady flier died in a crash in Chicago to-day. Labor day. She was a daughter of Mr. and Mrs. Gus Sunderson of

September 14, 1932: We had a bad fire upstairs today. We had to run up the stairs and put it out with pails of water. Farmers have no fire protection.

September 30, 1932: Another bank robbery. This one was at Wahpeton, N.D.

November 8, 1932: Franklin Roosevelt elected President of the United States.

June 18, 1933: It was so hot today it was burning up the crop. We no longer get the Fargo Forum. Can't afford it.

February 1, 1935: Hillsboro has now shipped out 250 carloads of bailed hay to save the starving cows in Western North Dakota.

February 2, 1935: Governor Thomas Moodie was forced to resign because he had not been a North Dakota resident for the required five years. Governor William Langer was put out of office, charged with illegal money matters, seven months earlier.

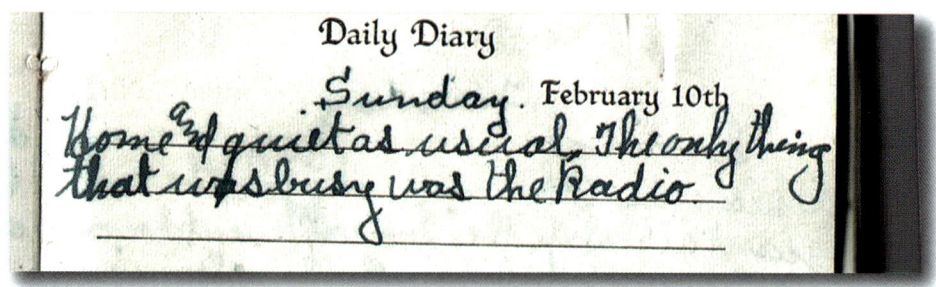

Daily Diary — Sunday, February 10th: Home and quiet as usual. The only thing that was busy was the Radio.

July 27, 1935: Rust has destroyed the wheat crop this year.

July 31, 1935: We all went to town to see "The First Commandment."

January 17, 1936: The body of Corporal Lynn Spiering, who was killed in France in World War I, was found and returned to Hillsboro, N.D.

May 9, 1939: UND and NDAC [now NDSU] students had a picnic in Hillsboro.

March 24, 1940: "Gone with the Wind" movie was shown in Fargo for $1.10.

June 1940: Tilford Aasen graduated from NDAC with a degree in engineering.

June 7, 1944: Baby pigs were born last night.

February 20, 1946: While milking, I was knocked down and kicked in the ribs. It hurts but I was lucky.

June 16, 1949: My mother died today on the farm. She was 90 and was never in a hospital.

Three
A Norwegian Bachelor Farmer

Garrison Keillor has often told stories about Norwegian bachelor farmers, and they are very funny. And true to life.

I know because I was raised by one in North Dakota in the 1930's. His name was Alfred Brenden, and he was my surrogate father and my uncle. When I was five years old, my Dad was killed in a car accident, and we moved to Alfred's farm. I grew up on that farm under the watchful eyes of my mother, two brothers, a grandmother and Uncle Alfred.

Alfred was over six feet tall, gangling, with blue eyes, big ears and very poor teeth. Old fashioned farmers in the 1930's did not believe in dentists — or could not afford them. Alfred was gruff, tough and he always got in the last word.

He wore bib overalls the year around. He also wore long john underwear all year, which puzzled me and my two older brothers. He didn't buy raincoats — probably because they were not very good anyway. And farmers are usually so happy when it rains that they ignore the weather!

Alfred was gruff but also very shy. That is probably the reason he remained a bachelor for 74 years. If we had female company, he would often remain in the barn, pretending he had something urgent to do there.

There were rumors that Alfred had known several of his hired girls very well. However these rumors were never documented.

We three boys — being curious — often went through his most personal possessions. We knew the most about his love life, but we never said a word.

Alfred, his mother, my mother and we three boys all lived on this big wheat farm with a lot of cows, chickens, pigs and eight horses. And hired men and hired "girls" (they were called) came and went all the time. There was more than enough work for all.

Alfred worked six days a week from early morning to late at night. He never took a vacation or a long trip, which he easily could have afforded. In his 74 years, he never got more than a couple of hundred miles from the farm he was born on. In those days you were not born in hospitals.

He rolled his own cigarettes most of the time. On Sunday, he might treat himself to a tailor-made Lucky Strike. He smoked Prince Albert, which came in a flat red tin that he always carried in a front pocket in his big overalls. A cigarette dangled from his lips most of the time, which may be the reason he died from mouth and throat cancer.

The Hard Stuff

He did not drink "the hard stuff," as they called it in those days. But he might have a few bottles of beer hidden in the bottom of the water trough that the horses and cows drank from. The artesian well brought the water up from far below and it kept his beer cool but not cold.

As modern farm machinery had not yet reached North Dakota, we always had a lot of hired men who slept in the barn on the hay. They drank the "hard stuff" which was alcohol bought from bootleggers. They drank it with hot water and sugar and it had a powerful kick. I think he never touched it because he had a big work crew and a lot of things on his mind and he didn't want to lose control. And the work crew could be a rough lot.

Alfred was a man of strong opinions and he was not reluctant to share them with you. He would start in the morning by attacking the Coca-Cola Company. We didn't know why he didn't like this company. Every time he saw one of their trucks on the highway, he would yell "There goes another of those damn Coke trucks." He didn't like "big business" and that may have been the reason for his strange behavior.

As the day wore on, he would continue his grousing and by nightfall he would be making critical comments about the U.S. government, most politicians and even the U.S. Supreme Court.

He apparently felt powerless against government and his special target was the U.S. Department of Agriculture. This is rather funny because he got checks from the Department every year he farmed! "They shouldn't stick their nose in my business," he would say. "If they know so much about farming, why don't they come out here to North Dakota and try it."

Another pet gripe of his was the elected officials who worked in the local county court house. "All they do is sit around in their white shirts and spit in their spittoons" he often charged. Despite my uncle's opinions, the county officials seemed to win most elections and were some of the few people in the thirties who had regular jobs.

Number one on his hate list was a local man who had caused a local bank to go under — and Alfred lost a lot of money. About once a day Alfred would say "…and that son of a bitch still sits in the front pew in church every Sunday."

A Lonely Job

Although he had his pet peeves, he liked most people and they liked him. He was regarded as an honest man who kept his word and paid his bills on time. There were not too many "Alfreds" in Depression days. But he was a lonely man in a very lonely business — farming. Far from town, he could work in the fields all day without seeing another human being. His best days were when he could stop the mailman for a visit or catch another farmer for a talk.

He was very good to us three kids, our mother and grandmother. In many families, it is the daughter who ends up taking care of their mother and the sons sidestep the responsibility. In our farm house, both the son and the daughter took care of our grandmother — their mother. In those days you didn't put old people in "rest" homes.

Alfred Brenden and I are oiling and greasing up a binder for cutting and binding wheat in this 1941 photo. Around this time, combines were actively replacing binders and threshing machines. Mechanization was radically changing farming.

Alfred loved horses, newborn calves and fields of waving wheat. He enjoyed spring the best because that is when the newborn calves would come out of the barn and wobble around the barnyard like they were trying out stilts.

Alfred was a very good farmer and he saved his money. The neighbors wondered who would get his money when he died. His only luxury was big cars. He always had either a Buick or a Studebaker. He confided one time that what he really wanted was a Cadillac. He could have paid cash for one, too. But he said, "The neighbors will think I am showing off." He took better care of his cars than he did of his teeth. Every Sunday he would wash and tinker with his car. For many years he went to a small, nearby Lutheran church (St. Olaf) on Sundays, but one day he stopped going forever. When asked why he quit going to church, he said "Their damn stove doesn't work right and every Sunday I had cold feet."

As he got older, more and more people would whisper, "Who is going to get all that money. He must have a fortune." In those days in North Dakota, it did not take much money to be considered a "fortune."

After Alfred died a painful death from cancer, my oldest brother was going through his personal trunk. He found a will that Alfred had written in his own handwriting. The lawyers called it a "holographic" will, which is good in some states but not in others.

The court ruled it was legal. His money would go where he wanted it to go. Nobody was going to tell him anything!

He was, after all, a regular Norwegian bachelor farmer who kept his own counsel — and always had the last word!

Four
GOING TO SCHOOL

A one-room schoolhouse

The River School was in Noble Township, Cass County, N.D., five miles from Gardner, N.D., and 10 miles from Perley, Minn. It had only one room, no basement, and no bathrooms. Two little outhouses were needed. One-room schools were used in North Dakota from around the turn of the century through the 1930's.

Five local men, all farmers, had control of the school including hiring the teacher, ordering the books, and making sure there was enough coal to keep the school warm. Some schools may have been heated by wood.

Teachers got paid for teaching but they had many other jobs. They had to be the janitor, disciplinarian, nurse, referee, and more. They roomed in a local family's house, or slept right in their school building. As a rule, no one else lived near the school and some teachers worried about security. The pay was very low.

And if they smoked, used lipstick or got married, they were fired.

This building replaced the old River School and it was a very big improvement.

It had a big basement where the kids could play in the winter and parents could hold square dances. There was a small kitchen where the students could warm up their food. The seats were bolted down and it was a no-no to play with the ink well in each desk. Teaching many age groups was difficult because the young kids could hear the older kids' lessons and vice versa.

These kids sure look like they love their school. It was called Eldorado #5, located near Taft, North Dakota.

Fathers loved to tell their kids how they walked three miles to school every day. Now for a true story: We kids walked one mile a day to school. The boys gave their lunch boxes to the girls to carry so they could throw snowballs, fight, and do boy things. I know this is true, since I was one of the boys.

Most children walked to school in warm weather.

These smiling third graders, wearing warm caps, coats and boots were not bothered by the North Dakota weather. "Bring it on," they seem to say---and never give up!

These are the Johnson kids. This photo records a happy day in 1922. Note the ties and hats.

This picture also tells a story. These kids may have all been in different classes, but a teacher in a one-room school had to sort them out by grade! The teacher had a hard time developing proper instruction for students ranging in age from five to fifteen or so.

Five
Farm Kids

Farm kids did not have the conveniences available to town kids but they probably had some fun that town kids did not. They could play in barns, ride horses (or sheep) and build shacks in the woods.

"There is nobody in this chicken coop but us chickens." Four cousins act out an old joke that I must have heard many times.

The author (left) with his friend David Sayre in a pool hall in 1940. From 1900 to 1940, pool halls were popular places for young men and boys in North Dakota towns. Some considered them to be sinful places, where idle youth wasted time and smoked cigarettes. A well known church leader in the early 1940's used his radio program to urge North Dakota's fine young men to stay out of the smoky pool halls and stinking beer halls. Considering the popularity of the halls, it does not seem that his advice was followed.

As the boys got older, their wagons got bigger. Above, kids would give each other a ride. Below, kids could ride in a wagon pulled by a horse wearing a blanket for protection against mosquitos.

In the fall, North Dakota fields used to be covered with straw stacks about 20 feet high. As North Dakota is mostly flat, the kids realized that the stacks could be used as ski slides after it snowed. For many years these stacks provided a lot of downhill (down straw?) fun. Some little jumps were added at the bottom of the slide so the kids could compete in jumping contests.

Today straw is scattered on the fields by combines; the straw stacks are gone.

For fun, all you need is a bike...and a brother.

Clarice Johnson, age two, from Cass County, N.D., enjoys her dolls.

My son, David, swung on hay ropes in the old barn in the late 1960's, just like we did.

Six
WEATHER

No story about North Dakota would be complete if it didn't comment on the weather.

This photograph of the Nora Church near Gardner, N.D., during the flood of 1935 tells one story.

The aerial view of Grand Forks (to the right) during the catastrophic flood of 1997 tells a wetter story. This was the most severe flooding of the Red River since 1826.

Flood waters inundated Grand Forks, N.D., and East Grand Forks, Minn. The picture is looking west to Grand Forks. Photo by Tony Mutzenberger, U.S. Geological Survey. Public domain.

And every year, of course, brings its share of snow.

This Whippet was left outsde during a snowstorm near Fargo in 1930.

This photograph shows what might be a one-story house. But it is a two-story house in deep North Dakota snow.

Seven
FAMILY SIZE

North Dakota families were generally larger than families throughout the United States until after 1960. This family includes six children. Source: State Historical Society of North Dakota

North Dakota has gone from big families on small farms to mostly small families on large farms today. In 1890, the average farm was about 277 acres. Today the average size is 1,312 acres, according to North Dakota Blue Books.

And, according to ND.Gov, in 1920 there were 4.8 people in the average North Dakota family, higher than the national average of 4.3 people. In 2010, the average North Dakota family was about 2.29 people, slightly lower than the national average of 2.55.

The average North Dakota family was indeed likely to live on a farm right up until 1990 when the balance shifted, and more people lived in cities and towns than on farms (according to ND.Gov).

This article originally appeared in North Dakota Horizons (Spring 2013).

PIONEER FAMILY RETROSPECTIVE
Size Of Families And Farms Impact North Dakota Life
By Larry Aasen

North Dakota has gone from big families on small farms in the 1920's to mostly small families on large farms today. In 1890, the average farm was about 277 acres. Today the average size is 1,283 acres, according to North Dakota Blue Books. It is impossible to give the average number of children then and now. But most North Dakotans agree we have gone from large families to smaller families. Just looking at old family pictures and current ones can indicate how family sizes have changed.

Henry and Clara Johnson raised their family of 11 children on a small farm near Gardner, about 20 miles from Fargo. This farm family symbolizes economic and social trends in the 1920's and 1930's in North Dakota.

The Henry Johnson family, pictured on the adjacent page, is a good example of a large family in the 1900's. They lived in Noble Township, Cass County, east of Gardner and across the Red River from Perley, Minnesota. They raised 11 children on a farm of about 350 acres. Those children are my first cousins. My dad was Mrs. Clara Johnson's brother.

Families lives span a century.

The lives of the 11 Johnson children span more than a hundred years. The first and oldest Johnson child, Arnold was born in 1902; the youngest and last child, Inez Johnson Oien, was born in 1926. All of these children grew up on the farm and all went on to be hard working, respected citizens. Except for one bachelor, all married and had children. They all ended up living in the North Dakota and Minnesota area except for Sanford and Edna, who went to California. In their younger days, the Johnsons spent few, if any days, in hospitals. When Inez Johnson Oien died in Columbus Heights, Minn., on May 10, 2011, all the Henry Johnson children were gone.

On their small farm the Johnsons raised wheat, barley, oats, corn, and flax. Selling these crops in the fall was the major source of their income. Some money was made by selling eggs and cream in their closest town, Perley, Minn. In the wintertime the Johnson brothers made some money hunting and trapping raccoons, weasels, fox and mink. For obvious reasons, they didn't bother much with all the skunks around. Some cash was also earned by working for neighbor farmers. The Johnsons purchased very little from the stores in Perley or Fargo. They made some of their clothes and ordered most of the others from mail order catalogues, Sears Roebuck and Montgomery Ward.

The Johnson's big garden and their livestock put food on the table. The cows provided milk, butter, cheese. Some cows and calves were sold to local butchers. Bulls were shared with neighbors. Produce from the garden, meatballs and beef slices were put up in glass jars and stored in the root cellar for winter eating.

At the Johnson house, pancakes were served every day. Henry would get up before the rest of the family and get the pancakes started. When they were ready, he lifted up a big pan and banged very hard on it with a big metal spoon. It worked. The family would soon gather at the long kitchen table.

The Johnson's eight horses provided the energy to pull the farm machinery. Sometime in the 1920's, they brought their first tractor. If the farmers today could see how the land was farmed in those days, they would not believe it. Just as the farmers of yesterday would not believe the way farming is done today.

Buggies came before cars.

Before cars came to the farm in the 1920's, buggies had been the means of travel. The Johnson boys, as they were called, all had cars, mostly used Model T's. The yard in front of the Johnson house often looked like a parking lot. As farmers by necessity work with machinery, they are often good mechanics. The Johnson boys could take a Model T apart and put it back together, fast and efficiently. Very few cars went to the repair shop in Perley. Almost all of the roads were dirt or gravel. Snow, mud and ice provided a constant challenge.

The Johnson children attended the one-room school house near the farm. One teacher taught all eight grades. Her other duties were to be janitor, nurse, referee, and to take care of anything else that came up during the day. A large coal stove provided the heat in the winter. The outhouse sat back behind the school house. Portraits of Washington and Lincoln looked down on the students. Most of the teachers had two years of education at a teacher's college. Usually the teachers taught for about two years and then got married, often to a local farmer, or took a new job, hopefully in town. Teaching in a rural school was a lonely, difficult life with very low pay.

Finishing school in Fargo.

The Johnson family had four girls and seven boys. After finishing eight grades in the little country school the Johnson girls roomed with families in Fargo so they could go to high school. The boys were needed on the farm and there was little opportunity for them to go to high school. Leonard Johnson, however, did graduate from Hendrum (Minn.) High School and then from the Dakota Business School in Fargo.

There were some advantages in being born in a large family like the Johnsons. Clothes and schoolbooks could be passed down the line. There was no need for babysitters. The oldest children took care of the younger ones. Very few hired men were needed on the farm, as the sons, starting at about age 12, were required to join the work force. The year-round playground was the hayloft in the barn. In the summer, the pasture became the baseball field.

Henry Johnson, born in 1876, was a good farmer, a quiet, dignified man who ruled his large family by gentle prodding, no physical punishment. Henry served on the school board for the local school. In those days, the board kept close watch on the teacher so that she (seldom a "he") behaved. The teachers were held to high standards, including no drinking, smoking, lipstick, and modest clothing. Parents watched the teacher very closely to make sure their children were not corrupted.

Clara Johnson, born in 1882, worked from morning to night, taking care of her 11 children, working in the large garden, washing clothes by hand, and canning food to be eaten during the long winters. She was an active member of the Nora Lutheran Church and made all the kids go to Sunday school. All were confirmed in Nora.

A way of life gone forever.

Clara Johnson's main social activities were the church's Ladies Aid meetings, the local Homemaker's Club and visiting with relatives and neighbors. The one hour a week she spent in church was probably the only time she could rest and relax. Clara's love was babies and children, and her 11 kids knew that. When other kids would visit the Johnsons, Clara always had a candy sucker for each one.

The Johnson house was large. Henry and Clara slept in a bedroom on the main floor and all the kids found their sleeping space upstairs. A large coal stove and a kitchen wood stove provided heat. Kerosene lamps and lanterns provided the light. The communication was by telephone. During the Depression, some farm families could not afford the telephone. They got their news from the radio, mostly WDAY, and the Fargo Forum newspaper.

The Johnson family represented a way of life that is gone forever. Henry, Clara and their children have passed on. Four generations of Johnsons are buried in the Nora Church Cemetery. The farmland is still owned by Carl's family.

But, there is hardly a trace of the old Johnson family farm. It is now a plowed field. A few trees remain. But all the cows, horses and buildings are gone. The one-room schoolhouse is gone. The Johnson family era is history.

This article was written with assistance from Tom and Cay Pierce and Allan and Ona Ellenson.

Eight
GOING TO NDAC (1941-1943)

Entrance to Agricultural College, Fargo, N.D

The bill founding North Dakota Agricultural College (NDAC) was signed on March 8, 1890, seven years after initial plans to start an agricultural college in the northern portion of the Dakota Territory. NDAC was established as a land-grant university. It continued to grow and was renamed North Dakota State University (NDSU) on November 8, 1960 after a statewide referendum.

In 1993 the NDSU Alumni Office asked alumni a series of questions. Here are some of them, and my responses.

What was your favorite campus activity?

ROTC rifle team shooting. It was 1941 and we listened constantly to the war news from Europe. TV had not yet arrived. We were shocked on that Sunday when we heard that Pearl Harbor had been bombed. The first thing we did was hunt for an atlas so we could find out where Pearl Harbor was. We had never heard of it.

Some of us wore our ROTC uniforms to attract attention on campus. Rural and town kids really went through the same events.

Did you have a job?

I had a job at the North Dakota Correspondence School doing odd jobs — like filing. I got 25 cents an hour from the National Youth Administration (NYA). I was very happy to get it.

What former classmates would you like to see at the reunion?

As I am 96, the ones I remember are gone. We ate our meals in the basement of the Men's Residence Hall. We cooked our own meals and it was a fun event.

What was your most cherished memory of NDAC?

The end of the semester when I found out that I had not flunked out. I loved the brisk, beautiful Saturdays at the football stadium. Those big, thick milk shakes they sold downtown. The kind professors who knew that some of us were not ready for college — but didn't tell. Getting a ride as we tried to hitchhike home — competing with other students who had the same idea.

Pranks or events that you wish to admit or recall?

We knew that a war was near and we knew that some students would be drafted. We didn't dare to pull any pranks or fool around because our Draft Board might hear about it. We drank a little beer, but I cannot remember ever drinking the "hard stuff." We were too broke to afford it.

A true story

Clara Aasen, my mother, attended NDAC briefly in the early 1890's. She stayed in a girls' dormitory which was ruled by a house mother (also called the "Matron"). Often the house mother, who hated cobwebs, would go down the hallways with a broom, singing "the beaus won't go where the cobwebs grow."

NDAC Will Continue Despite Government Action

THE SPECTRUM

Vol. LVII Z 545a State College Station, North Dakota, Friday, December 18, 1942 Number 11

Eversull Declares College Possibly Among Schools Named For Military Setup

"There will always be an AC, ROTC and an OCS."

With these words NDAC's president, Dr. Frank L. Eversull, bluntly stated the circumstances under which the college will function following the Washington announcement Thursday of a joint program by the Army, Navy, Marine Corps and Coast Guard for the utilization of the country's collegiate educational facilities.

Speaking at a special convocation called in Festival hall Thursday at 4, Dr. Eversull stressed the importance of students returning for the winter term if at all possible. Regardless of what action is finally taken by the armed services in utilizing NDAC facilities, Dr. Eversull declared that college classes would continue to operate for women students and those men students not effected by the new regulations.

Dr. Longwell Addresses 21 Graduates

Dr. J. H. Longwell, chief of the Division of Animal Industry, will address 21 candidates for bachelor of science degrees at the fall term commencement exercises to be held this afternoon at 3 in Festival Hall. His topic will be, "Is It Worth The Cost?"

Degrees will be conferred by President Frank L. Eversull. Lt.-Col. Charles H. Hart, Jr., ROTC commandant, will present commissions to two seniors.

With final grades still to be reported to the office of Registrar A. H. Parrott, the following candidates were approved this week by the College Council.

EIGHT AGS

Students from the School of Agriculture are the most numerous among this fall's graduates with eight candidates to be presented. They are David Askegaard, Orville Block, Lelan Good, Daniel Gust, Arley Hovland, Christian Naaden, Lester Markusen and Harold Solberg.

Seven students will receive degrees from the School of Engineering include William Ackerman, Melvin Anderson, Arnold Besserud, Carroll Elan, Vernon Peterson, Carl Eicholm and Francis Smylie.

AA&S HAS FOUR

Kenneth Christenson, Charles Cadieux, Walter Maddock and Rolfe Tainter will be the candidates from the School of Applied Arts and Sciences while one senior, Marion Schmitt, will graduate from the Division of Education.

Florence Mickelson is the only candidate from the School of Home Economics.

Col. Hart will present commissions as second lieutenants in the Army of the United States to Askegaard and Naaden.

Three Cadets Get ROTC Rankings At Tuesday Parade

Three ROTC seniors received their commissions in the NDAC cadet regiment at the fall term graduation parade held Tuesday afternoon in the Fieldhouse.

Commissioned by President Frank L. Eversull were Cadet Lt.-Col. Kenneth Stamus, Cadet Maj. David Askegaard and Cadet Capt. Christian Naaden. Lt.-Col. Charles H. Hart, Jr., professor of military science and tactics, presented the trio with crossed rifles and gold bars.

Askegaard and Naaden will be commissioned as second lieutenants in the Army of the United States at commencement exercises this afternoon while Stamus will receive his army commission after completing an officer candidate course.

WE APOLOGIZE

Beverly Halbeisen's name was unintentionally omitted from the list of Edwin Booth initiates in last week's Spectrum.

Board Action Cancels 1943 Bison Yearbook

There will be no 1943 Bison yearbook. Action to this effect was swiftly taken Thursday afternoon at a special meeting of the Board of Publications Control.

Uncertainty as to the size of the enrollment of students at NDAC during the winter and spring quarters prompted the action by the board.

Advertising contracts and other business transactions will be cleaned up as soon as possible, announces Business Manager Vincent Mayoue. Glenn Gullickson was editor of the now cancelled publication.

January issues of the Bison Burrows and North Dakota State Engineer will be published with action on future issues to be taken following the holiday recess.

Spectrum publication is not effected by the board action and will continue.

Merry Christmas and Happy New Year!

Hart Announces Non-Coms For ROTC Cadet Regiment

Non-commissioned officers of the NDAC Cadet Corps have been announced by Lt.-Col. Charles H. Hart, professor of Military Science and Tactics. They include:

Company A—
First Sergeant Richard T. Carley; Platoon guide: Frank O. Bauman, 1st Pl.; Neil E. Bergquist, 2nd Pl.; Donald E. Brockel, 3rd Pl.; Platoon Sergeants: Royal R. Berstler, 1st Pl.; William E. Anderson, 2nd Pl.; William K. Barner, 3rd Pl.

Company B—
First Sergeant, Waldo A. Gerlitz; Platoon guides: Dell M. Colwell, 1st Pl.; John J. Dwyer, 2nd Pl.; Lloyd O. Holm, 3rd Pl.; Platoon Sergeants: William J. Carlisle, 1st Pl.; Ray W. Gordon, 2nd Pl.; Ernest C. Hector, 3rd Pl.

Company C—
First Sergeant, Samuel B. Hess. Platoon guides: Lauren B. Johnson, 1st Pl.; John Kingsett, 2nd Pl.; Harvey J. Krogh; Platoon Sergeants: Melvin E. Holmquist, 1st Pl.; Bruce E. Hoverson, 2nd Pl.; William S. Klubben, 3rd Pl.

Company E—
First Sergeant, Robert C. Lambourn; Platoon guides: Earl H. Leland, 1st Pl.; William O. Lund, 2nd Pl.; Ellsworth A. Moe, 3rd Pl.

Platoon Sergeants: John W. Lytle, 1st Pl.; George A. Martin, 2nd Pl.; Arvid I. Melby, 3rd Pl.

Company F—
First Sergeant, Arnold J. Stockstad. Platoon guides: John E. Rilling, 1st Pl.; Thomas M. Sakshaug, 2nd Pl.; Delbert Sand, 3rd Pl. Platoon Sergeants: James A. Poseley, 1st Pl.; Clifford C. Rothrock, 2nd Pl.; Darrel Sand, 3rd Pl.

Company G—
First Sergeant, Earl E. Walter; Platoon guides: Don R. Swenson, 1st Pl.; Russell Thompson, 2nd Pl. Platoon Sergeants: Theodore S. Thompson, 1st Pl.; Vilas T. Walhood, 2nd Pl.

Lovsness Goes To Army Duty In Arkansas

Maj. Neal W. Lovsness, instructor in military science and tactics at NDAC since September, 1940, has been ordered to active duty at Camp Joseph T. Robinson, Little Rock, Ark., announces Lt.-Col. Charles H. Hart, Jr., ROTC commandant.

Major Lovsness, a graduate of NDAC, will report to his new post January 15 and will be replaced here by Second Lieutenant Howard C. Olson of the 77th Division, Fort Jackson, S. C. Lt. Olson also is a graduate of NDAC.

Tryota Club Tackles Man-size Work In Silk Salvage Job

It's a man-sized job, this gathering of silk and nylon stockings to be turned over to the government for use as powder bags by the army.

But——the women are doing it! Yes, sir. The Tryota Club, with Lillian McDowall as chairman of the drive, is asking all NDAC co-eds to bring old, clean silk and nylon hose to Ceres Hall where facilities for collection have been arranged.

Do it today, gals! It all goes for a worthy cause.

Blue Belles To Be Vogue At All-College

Who will be the first Belle of the Blue Key Ball?

This question will be high in the minds of NDAC students during Christmas vacation.

The belle will be elected at the Blue Key annual all-college dance to be held in Festival Hall during the winter quarter.

All sororities, Ceres Hall, and the ISA will nominate 2 candidates for the honor.

Blue Key will then select one candidate to represent each group.

These girls will be rated upon by the student body at the dance.

During the dance the University Blue Key chapter will formally return the traveling nickel trophy to NDAC.

This trophy goes to the school winning the annual University-AC football contest.

COLLABORATED PROGRAM

Thursday's announcement from Washington is the publicizing of a program which was first considered last October and which military and educational leaders have been collaborating on since that time.

Members of the armed services, including draftees of the 18- and 19-year-old age group and students now in college will be eligible for the new training program.

MUST BE EQUIPPED

Dr. Eversull declared that screening tests will be given to the newly enrolled soldier to determine whether he is "intellectually, temperamentally, physiologically and educationally equipped to withstand the rigid requirements needed to complete the planned courses." A four-year college course will be scheduled in a period of two calendar years.

Those found qualified during their basic training period will be sent to college for specialized training but will be returned to combat units as soon as it is found that they are not maintaining the proper scholastic standards.

ARMY RESERVES CALL

All members of the Army Enlisted Reserve will be called to active duty after the first of the year and may then be returned to college to continue work in specialized fields. Senior ROTC men will complete their work at NDAC before attending their service branch school and receiving their commissions.

Students enrolled in the Navy's reserve programs, according to the present schedule, will have a fine chance of completing their college training uninterrupted although they may be placed in an active status before their training is finished.

Senior Staff Sets All-College Dance

Members of Senior Staff announce the second all-college dance of the school year sponsored by that group to be held Jan. 10 in the Fieldhouse. President Jean Hoeft says that as yet a band has not been signed for the party.

Charlotte Bahe is in charge of musical arrangements while Betty Lynne and Mildred Strong handling ticket sales. Annabelle Donovan and Marjorie Nees Lindemann are on the chaperon committee.

Three Named By Alpha Zeta

Dacotah chapter of Alpha Zeta, national honorary agricultural fraternity, recently elected the following men to membership.

LeRoy Noyes
Earl Walter
Arnold Stockstad

Selection is based upon scholarship, leadership and character.

The management and employees of the Powers Coffee Shop join in wishing you all

A Merry Christmas

Front page of *The Spectrum*, NDAC student newspaper, December 18, 1942. Even on campus, WWII dominated the news. In the lead story, NDAC President Frank L. Eversull reassured students that the college would continue to operate even while contributing to the war effort. In North Dakota, college presidents don't give up. Copyright © by The Spectrum of NDSU. Reprinted with permission.

The NDSU Class of 1943 meets in 1992 *(photo at right)*:

Front (L to R): Russ Burfening, Howard Cole. Charles Friese, Pat Torgerson Berg, Francis Daniel, Larry Aasen.

Row 2: John Finnie, Janet Peterson Culpepper, Lorraine Brevik Johnson, Mildred Duckstad Sloan (black & white), Bernice Wichman Benson (tan), Paul Huss.

Row 3: Earl Shaw, Shirley Soliah Michel, Pat Bjorklund Phillips, Jim Ford, Leland Brand (tan with glasses), Donald Bates.

Row 4: Mary Jane Pavlik Grieve (blue with glasses), Bette Eckre Johnson (dark glasses, blue vest), Ted Brevik (red tie), Dona Thompson Brevik, Eileen Osking Mork (red).

Row 5: Lois Skadeland Miller (floral), Audrey Jacobsen Eckert, Joe Dordahl, Paul Berge, Jim Noonan (light blue), Byron Smith (grey tweed).

Row 6: Ione Erickson Ford, Mildred Strong Bean, Don Gabe (tan), Henry Alquist, Bob Pile (navy, no tie), Eileen Dolve Larson, Joseph Larson

Row 7: Mina Askegaard Qualley, Doris Selvig Flaming, Jean Hoeft Bolz.

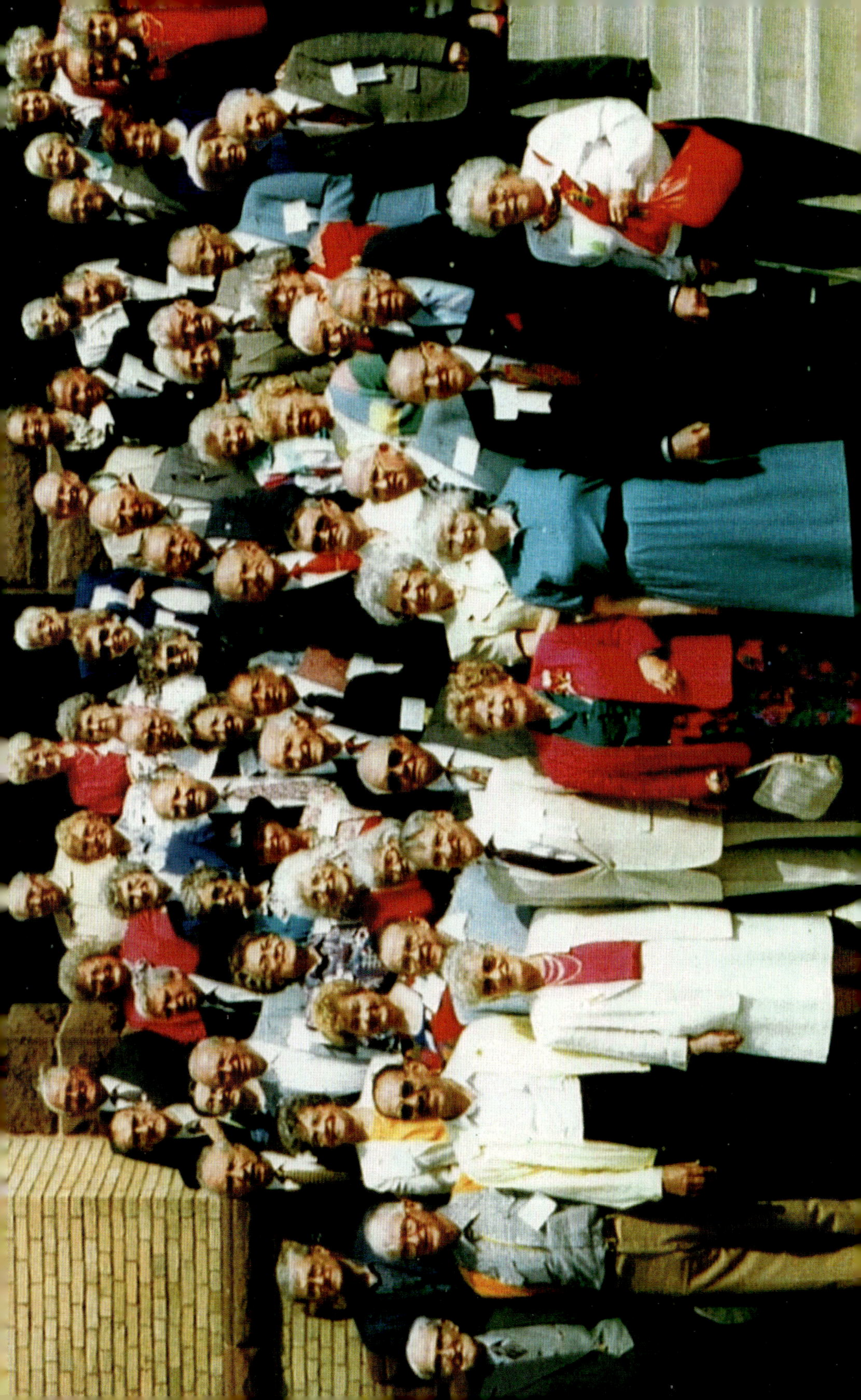

The ROTC unit at NDAC trained men to accept responsibility as reserve officers.

Dr. Frank L. Eversull was named President of NDAC in 1936. He had a doctorate in school administration from Yale University and had been President of Huron (S.D.) College.

Dr. Clarence Putnam led the NDAC Gold Star Band for 39 years. The 1942 Bison yearbook states that "the little brick hall on Festival Drive really begins to shift" when he gets his musicians "a jivin.'"

Nine
GOING TO UND

UND in the 1940's and the War Years

My first few days at UND were spent sleeping in some discarded Great Northern boxcars in Grand Forks, North Dakota. This was during the Depression so where we slept was known as "Camp Depression." At this point UND had very limited dormitory space. Later I was lucky to get a small room at Budge Hall, now gone. But I had to share the small room with two other students. As three could not study at the same desk, two had to go to the library.

The years 1942-1943 were tense, nervous years at UND. The main topic of conversation among the male students was "THE DRAFT." Every day we would hear about some students who had been drafted. We wondered when our name would come up.

Under those conditions it was very difficult to concentrate on study. Veterans, who had been in a lot of combat, could not sit still for an hour in class. Most graduated, but they had a rough

WHITEY'S CAFE

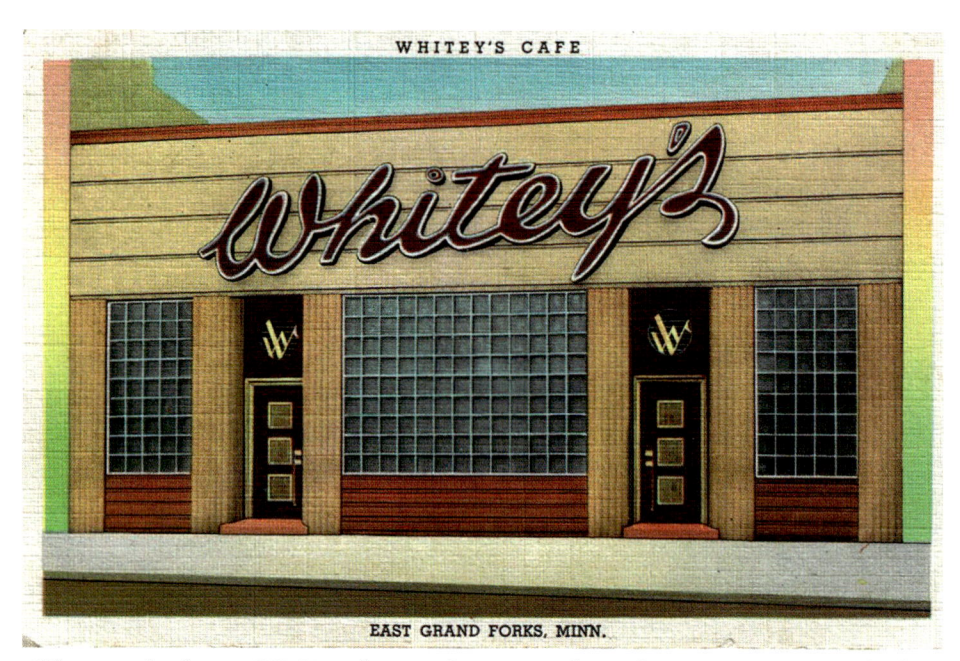

EAST GRAND FORKS, MINN.

If you asked any UND alum what was their favorite watering hole in Grand Forks, they would say "Whitey's."

time. I remember the dark mood on the campus when we got word that the first UND student had been killed in WWII.

There was very little interest in national politics on campus, but one day North Dakota Senator Gerald P. Nye visited UND. He attracted national attention because he had been against the war. He said we should organize a "Young Republicans" club on campus and some students did.

UND had dances with fun names like: The Spinster Skip, The Sweetheart Ball, Flickertail Follies and The Shadow Ball. Each year the sororities elected the "Best Looking" man on campus. Those elections were disbanded because of voter fraud. Fraternities and sororities were very popular and the "independent" students often felt left out of campus life. The athletes stuck together in the UND football stadium. The journalists made up another clique on campus and they bonded as they worked into the night to get the Dakota Student out. Sometimes the administration did not applaud the newspaper!

A very big man headed the music department for many years. A campus joke was that you could never see the band when conductor John Howard stood in front of the players.

The high points of the school year were the days when UND would play NDAC (now NDSU) in the UND football stadium. All of North Dakota listened to these games on the radio; TV had not yet arrived. Two of the outstanding football players in 1939 were Ernie Wheeler of NDAC and Fritz Pollard of UND. Hockey came to UND in 1947 and many of the players were from Canada.

Notables of UND

Fritz Pollard Jr.

Fritz Pollard has often been referred to as the greatest athlete that has ever played for UND. He starred in football, track and boxing. To keep in good shape during the winters in North Dakota, he would run on the top of railroad boxcars, hurtling over the gaps between them.

He was born in Springfield, Mass., the son of Fritz Pollard, Sr., also a fine athlete. Pollard enrolled at UND in 1935. He was invited to join his close friend Jesse Owens on the 1936 Olympic Track and Field team. Pollard took home a bronze medal in the 110-meter hurdles despite tripping over the next-to-last hurdle.

Pollard was one of the school's first African-American graduates, leaving UND with a bachelor's degree in education. He later earned a law degree from the John Marshall Law School. He was a special services officer during World War II and later a teacher in Chicago and a Foreign Service officer in the State Department. HE NEVER GAVE UP.

Fritz Pollard

John Hancock

John Hancock

John Milton Hancock was a big man. Big in business, big personality and a big donor to UND. Hancock was born February 2, 1883 in Emerado, North Dakota. His father was a farmer, a partner at a hardware store, and a realtor. Hancock graduated from UND in 1903. At UND he participated in football and track and was active in A.D.T., a literary society, and served as editor of The Dakota Student.

Hancock served in China during World War I. After the war, he served in many important Navy jobs, twice working with Franklin Roosevelt, who was then Assistant Secretary of the Navy. In 1946-1947 he worked with Bernard Baruch on the U.S. Delegation to the United Nations Atomic Energy Commission.

Hancock joined the investment banking firm Lehman Brothers where he oversaw the resuscitation of the Jewel Tea Company in Chicago. He served as its president, and became the first partner at Lehman Brothers who was not a family member.

In this limited space it is impossible to list Hancock's success in the Navy, government and finance. His long resume records the enormously tangled tasks he faced for many years, BUT HE NEVER GAVE UP.

Chester Fritz

Chester Fritz was an investor who made a fortune in metals and silver in China. He was also a polo player, a horse racing competitor and a mountain climber. His mother was a French Canadian and his father a German. His father was disabled in a farm threshing accident in 1902. His mother left the family and was never seen again. The family was very poor.

Fritz attended UND for three years and graduated from the University of Washington in 1941.

After working at a west coast flour mill, he went to Hong Kong where he would live for 36 years. He climbed Mount Fuji, and entered horse riding contests. He created an investment firm called Swan, Culbertson and Fritz. Fritz often said that working in China in the 1930's was no picnic.

Fritz was good-looking, short, blunt and trim — an impressive and no-nonsense businessman.

He was married twice but had no children. His first wife was American journalist Bernadine Szold, whom he married in 1929 and divorced in 1946. He married again, to Vera Kachalina, a ballerina who studied at the Bolshoi. She died in 2005 and is buried next to Chester Fritz at the Grand Forks Memorial Park Cemetery.

Chester Fritz had fond memories of his time at UND, which he proved by giving two buildings and more to the university.

Despite his very humble, sad and confusing youth, and one bankruptcy, HE NEVER GAVE UP.

Chester Fritz

President John C. West

A very popular university president was John C. West. His presidency spanned the Great Depression, World War II, and the beginning of the Cold War. His financial acumen aided him in dealing with drastic budget cuts and salary reductions of the Depression.

After 21 years of service, he retired in 1954. He guided UND through tumultuous times, expanded the institution in "bricks and mortar," and developed research programs, all while maintaining relative harmony. HE NEVER GAVE UP!

The day I graduated he came over and hugged my mother. She never forgot that. The day West retired he said, "Now I put down the plow and pick up my fiddle and bow."

John C. West

Ten
WORLD WAR II

It was a cold and sad day on February 26, 1941, when National Guard Company L got on the train in Hillsboro, N.D., and left for Camp Claiborne in Louisiana. The company had been called to duty — like other North Dakota companies — because the army needed trained soldiers. Soldiers from all over Traill County belonged to Hillsboro's Company L. Many of them had never been more than 100 miles from home.

They were then shipped to the South Pacific, where they fought the Japanese at Guadalcanal and Bougainville. Other North Dakota towns with soldiers in the 164th regiment included Bismarck, Fargo, Devils Lake, Harvey, Bottineau, Cavalier, Grafton, Rugby, Cando, Williston, Carrington, Valley City, Jamestown, Edgeley, Wahpeton, Dickinson, Grand Forks and Hillsboro.

Many did not come home. North Dakota casualties in World War II were 1009 killed in action. 157 were wounded and later died. Ninety were missing in action, according to North Dakota records.

Capt. George "Jug" Newgard

The war changed many things. Young men were going into the army and there were few to fill local jobs, especially in farming. Some farmers were able to get German prisoners to do farm work.

In 2002, NDSU hosted a special reunion in honor of World War II veterans. One of those honored was **Capt. George "Jug" Newgard**, BS '28. Newgard had been the football, track and basketball coach at Hillsboro (N.D.) High School from 1928 to 1940.

A letter written for the occasion said "Many people have tried to define leadership. It is hard to define. But everybody agreed that Jug Newgard had it. He proved this not only as a high school coach and teacher. He also was respected for his leadership as captain of Hillsboro's Company L that got called into action in 1940.

"He never had to say much, never yelled, was always a gentleman, but he didn't miss anything. He was the kind of guy you would turn to when things were going wrong and say 'Jug, what should we do?' He knew what to do. If you talked to those still alive who played sports for Jug, you would not get a negative vote."

Newgard was killed in action on Guadalcanal, October 18, 1942. It was the first major offensive by Allied forces against the Empire of Japan. But he will be remembered by many Hillsboro High School graduates whose lives he touched.

Lynn W. Aas

Honored War Heroes

Lynn W. Aas DID NOT GIVE UP.

Aas, a World War II veteran from Minot, received **The Knight of the Legion of Honor Medal,** the highest award of the French government. It was awarded in recognition of his extraordinary bravery in helping to liberate France. Its recipients are named by a decree signed by the President of the Republic. He has also received the Bronze Star and the Purple Heart.

The medal was presented to Aas in 2017 by the consul general of France in a ceremony attended by North Dakota's two U.S. Senators, its U.S. Congressman and its governor.

Aas served in the Glider section of the 17th Airborne Division of the 193rd Airborne Infantry, which was in violent combat in the historic Battle of the Bulge. He has a hole in his field jacket that shows where a bullet went through. He was one of five soldiers of 500 who survived the battle that lasted 40 days. Aas landed in a combat area in a glider — one of the few American soldiers who did. He often had to sleep in a foxhole in deep snow.

After the war, he joined the Internal Revenue Service and served as a special investigator for ten years. At one time he was stationed in Brooklyn.

Aas has been active in politics in the Minot area for many years, serving as a member of the North Dakota Legislature during four sessions—1967, 1969, 1987, and 1989. He served as President of the Minot Chamber of Commerce and many local business, church and other organizations. Over the years he headed fund raising drives for many community groups.

Lynn's wife of 50 years died in 2003. They raised four sons, David (Kathy), Paul (Melodie), Daniel (Terry) and Joe (Nancy). Lynn has two sisters, Sally Graff of Sioux Falls and Helen Arntzen of Bottineau.

North Dakotan **Orville Emil Bloch** received the **Medal of Honor**. He joined the Army from Streeter, N.D., in February 1942. By September 1944 he was a first lieutenant in Company E, 338th Infantry Regiment, 85th Infantry Division. On that day, near Firenzuola, Italy, he led three soldiers in an attack on enemy positions which resulted in the capture of 19 prisoners and the silencing of five machine gun nests. For these actions, he was awarded the Medal of Honor on February 10, 1945.

Bloch's official Medal of Honor citation reads:

> For conspicuous gallantry and intrepidity at risk of life above and beyond the call of duty. 1st Lt. Bloch undertook the task of wiping out five enemy machine gun nests that had held up

the advance in that particular sector for one day. Gathering three volunteers from his platoon, the patrol snaked their way to a big rock, behind which a group of three buildings and five machine gun nests were located. Leaving the three men behind the rock, he attacked the first machine gun nest alone charging into furious automatic fire, kicking over the machine gun, and capturing the machine gun crew of 5. Pulling the pin from a grenade, he held it ready in his hand and dashed into the face of withering automatic fire toward this second enemy machine gun nest located at the corner of an adjacent building 15 yards distant. When within 20 feet of the machine gun he hurled the grenade, wounding the machine gunner, the other two members of the crew fleeing into a door of the house. Calling one of his volunteer group to accompany him, they advanced to the opposite end of the house, there contacting a machine gun crew of 5 running toward this house. 1st Lt Bloch and his men opened fire on the enemy crew, forcing them to abandon their machine gun and ammunition and flee into the same house. Without a moment's hesitation, 1st Lt. Bloch, unassisted, rushed through the door into a hail of small-arms fire, firing his carbine from the hip, and captured the seven occupants, wounding three of them. 1st Lt. Bloch with his men then proceeded to a third house where they discovered an abandoned enemy machine gun and detected another enemy machine gun nest at the next corner of the building. The crew of six spotted 1st Lt. Bloch the instant he saw them. Without a moment's hesitation he dashed toward them. The enemy fired pistols wildly in his direction and vanished through a door of the house, 1st Lt. Bloch following them through the door, firing his carbine from the hip, wounding two of the enemy and capturing six. Altogether 1st Lt. Bloch had single-handedly

1st Lt. Orville Bloch

captured 19 prisoners, wounding six of them and eliminating a total of five enemy machine gun nests. His gallant and heroic actions saved his company many casualties and permitted them to continue the attack with new inspiration and vigor.

Bloch later served in the Korean War, and reached the rank of colonel before retiring in 1970.

Letters from the Front

The following are excerpts from letters sent by a North Dakota soldier home to his mother in 1945:

February 8, 1945: "Censorship will make it hard to write long letters. You might want to re-read the letters my uncle sent home from France in WW-I. Many things have not changed in France. My uncle talked about railroad cars that would hold 40 men or 6 horses. We rode in those box cars yesterday. The toilets haven't changed much either."

February 27, 1945: "The barracks we are now in were used by the Germans when they were in France. The Germans wrote things on the walls like — 'The Truth is our greatest Weapon!' Some joke, heh. The poor French kids are always begging for cigarettes and chocolate. There is a terrific black market here. A pack of cigarettes = $2, a gallon of gas = $40."

April 17, 1945: "The French are really rough on the women who 'Collaborated' with the German soldiers. I saw one woman get all her hair cut off. Another woman was put in an old cart and dragged around town, with people jeering her."

June 21, 1945: "Today we went through the Maginot Line, built by the French at enormous expense. It is about 100 feet deep and is like a city under ground. Elaborate tunnels all over. I will never forget how proud our French guide was of the Maginot Line — one of the biggest military failures of all time. The Germans went over it and around it! Today the farmers are haying on top of it."

July 27, 1945: "The 13th Airborne Division is on its way home!!"

A farm crew during World War II shows age diversity. Three of the men were older than 70 and two were under 18. Melvin Eidem, second from left, was, like many in Traill County, called up by the National Guard.

War's impact remembered
Former ND man remembers how residents pitched in

Neighbors
By **Bob Lind**

These are difficult days for many people. But they were difficult 60-some years ago, too, whether you were in battle during World War II or toughing it out on the home front.

Larry Aasen saw the war from both angles.

Larry, now of Westport, Conn., grew up on a farm near Hillsboro, N.D., then served with the 13th Airborne Division in France from 1943 to 1946.

Thanks to his own memories and the diaries of his mother, Larry has many stories, and now he passes them on to Forum readers, starting with life on the farm.

Farmers were asked to produce more food than usual. But that was a good trick. For one thing, they had a hard time getting parts for their old machinery.

This article originally appeared in The Forum of Fargo-Moorhead on March 22, 2009. Reprinted with permission. Copyright © 2009 by The Forum of Fargo-Moorhead.

For another, most farm hands were in the service.

"The workers who were available were above the draft age and many were too old to be much help," Larry says.

Colleges let students have time off to work on farms, though, and prisoners of war were sent to area camps so they could work the fields. (*Neighbors* carried a story in 2008 about a camp in Moorhead for German POWs.)

American soldiers also were sent to help farmers. Larry says some of them were stationed at Mayville, N.D., and were paid 60 cents an hour by the farmers.

The farmers' wives did their share, and then some. Besides looking after their houses, they also drove tractors, brought in the hay, milked cows. "They did not look like fashion models on the tractors in all the dirt and dust," Larry says, "and they missed their lipstick and dresses. But they were proud to show their husbands that 'Anything you can do, I can do better!'"

As for the wives and girlfriends of the men overseas, well, it was a lonely time; "It was not a period of parties and joy," Larry says.

For mothers whose sons were fighting in the war, it was a time of stress, of fear. Such was the case for Clara Aasen. Two of her boys were in France. Larry was one of them.

Good, bad news

"Every single day we hoped for a letter from home," Larry says. Due to censorship, however, the men couldn't write back about what was happening.

"One of my good friends was killed by a land mine in France," Larry says. "The Germans had buried land mines before they left for Germany. This kind of news never got in letters to home."

But he says the home front did a good job of providing clothing such as socks, mittens and scarves for the soldiers. "The Red Cross ladies gave us coffee and doughnuts and made us think of home," and "once in a while candy or ethnic food would reach us."

Another welcome treat was receiving the hometown newspaper. Through it, the troops could learn both who had been discharged from the military and who had been killed.

The newspaper also brought news about which girls had married (ouch!).

And sometimes the mail brought that most dreaded piece of mail — a "Dear John" letter.

But all in all, Larry says, "The folks back home in North Dakota did every thing they could to support the North Dakota men and women in the service."

They, like everyone in the nation, put up with rationing: four gallons of gas a week, sugar, nylons, tires, meat. And they bought War Bonds, collected money for the Red Cross and the USO, collected scrap metal to be turned into tanks and planes.

Also, Larry says, "When the soldiers came home on furlough, they were treated like the heroes they were.

"The troops on the front did North Dakota proud (while) the people on the home front did everything they could to win the war.

"And," Larry's letter almost shouts, "we won!"

Big thrill

Larry has this story, too, of "a thrill I will always remember."

It was the day in 1946 when he returned from France to his farm home at Hillsboro, hugged his family, and then noticed a switch on the wall. He flicked it. And lights came on.

While he was gone, electricity had arrived.

Eleven
CARS

The first auto in Fargo, 1897

Cars and railroads were needed to pull together a state that is 400 miles by 200 miles with towns far apart from each other. North Dakota fell in love with cars. They started to come into North Dakota in about 1897 and North Dakotans bought them as soon as they could find the money or the credit. Cars reduced their isolation and gave them mobility.

By 1900 there was a growing demand for better roads. The battle cry to Congress was, "Get the farmers out of the mud!" The roads improved when Henry Ford invented the Model T. Its widespread sales and pressure from drivers caught the attention of politicians and a big roadbuilding program was soon underway.

In 1913 there were 13,075 automobiles in North Dakota. Just seven years later, in 1920 there were 92,000, showing the soaring popularity of cars.

The cold winters were a challenge to car owners. But they did not give up!

Mrs. Torger Brenden, Hillsboro, N.D. inspects the three cars her sons had bought sometime in 1917. The sons were very proud of their cars and territorial about them. According to their sister, no one else was allowed to touch or drive them. Can you name the cars?

The Little Car That Wouldn't Give Up

The Whippet, made by Willys Overland from about 1927 to 1931 in Toledo, Ohio, deserves a short tribute. Named after a small, swift dog, the Whippet was a four-cylinder car that looked like a Model A Ford. It was once the cheapest car on the market — roughly $495.

Whippet boasted of its "finger tip control," meaning if you lifted up the horn, the car started; if you pushed it down, the horn sounded; if you turned it, your lights came on!

I've got a sentimental fondness for the Whippet because a 1929 model took my two brothers and me to grade school and high school in North Dakota—a drive of five miles. A five-mile drive in a North Dakota blizzard can be a long five miles.

In the winter we took both the Whippet's oil and battery into our farm kitchen at night. The Whippet would be driven into the barn. All this was done in hope the car would start in the morning. If it didn't, a team of horses would pull it to get it going.

As our mother was a widow on a limited income, we were admonished not to waste any gasoline. Therefore we charged five cents a ride for anybody who wanted a ride during the school noon hour. However, for obvious reasons, some high school girls got to ride free.

The cars today are so full of electronic gadgets, computer-like functions, that people are not allowed to touch them.

Our old Whippet was "user friendly." It had a vacuum tank system to furnish fuel to the carburetor. If you ran the carburetor dry the vacuum tank was dry, also. So, upon pouring gasoline into the main tank, one would expedite the refilling of the vacuum tank by placing your lips (yes, your lips) upon the gasoline tank's spout (remove cap) and blow...HARD. You would blow until you heard the gasoline trickle into the vacuum tank. Then you could start the Whippet and you were again "King of the Road." Of course, you might want to spit!

We would take the car apart once in a while. If it was a slow Sunday on the farm, we might take off the oil pan and check the connecting rods. We might take off the radiator to check for leaks. (It was said some farmers put flax in their radiators to stop leaks!) The Whippet was sturdy and faithful and served us for about 25 years, for over 100,000 miles.

—Tilford Aasen

The Aasen brothers and their 1929 Whippet in 1935. The car was put to use for 25 years and took them over 100,000 miles.

Twelve
Christmas

As Norwegians, Germans and Russians comprised the major ethnic groups in North Dakota at the turn of the 20th Century, many greeting cards were in their languages. These postcards are in Norwegian. Even Santa smoked in those days.

The high point of the winter was the Christmas season. It started when the cows and horses—and the people—started to get more food. The cows and horses would get more hay and ground oats. The people in our Norwegian community would start to enjoy delicacies like lutefisk, lefse, fattigman and krumkaker.

I remember Christmas on the farm in the 1930's as a wonderful break in what may have not been a very good year. Grasshoppers, dust storms and low prices do not make your parents very jolly

Postcards were often used as Christmas cards; many often greeted other holidays as well. As the copier machine had not been invented, few families sent out long Christmas letters — reporting all the wonderful achievements of each child.

and the kids pick this up very quickly.

The thing I remember most about the old Christmas period was that we made everything—the food, the toys, the decorations, the cards, the clothes, the quilts, the presents, etc. Why? Lack of cash and shopping malls. Everybody in the house would be making something for Christmas. And it took creativity to find the materials you needed!

The Christmas season started when our Christmas decorations — tired, flyspecked, but beautiful — would be put up around the living room.

About this time we would get our first Christmas card. We got very few, because most of our friends and family — unlike today — lived within ten miles of our farm, and they were not about to

German-Russian children kneeled before the veiled "Krischtkindl" on Christmas. The female masquerader carried a willow switch in one hand and a bag of sweets in the other.

waste money on such sentimentality. The few cards we received were admired, passed around and saved in the family albums.

Christmas also started when we ordered our toys from Sears Roebuck or Montgomery Ward. Many of the toys were made of wood and lasted a long time. On Christmas Eve we would hang up our stockings around the coal stove. Few North Dakota farmhouses had fireplaces. We never saw him, but Santa would come during the night. During the night, one brother might sneak a lump of coal into another brother's stocking. This could lead to a fight in the morning.

The Christmas season would also start for us three boys when our Lutheran Sunday School teacher would try again to drill the story of Christ's birth into our heads. It was a nice story, we liked it, but the part about frankincense and myrrh confused us. The part about the manger and the barn we understood. Barns, we knew!

Thirteen

THEY NEVER GAVE UP.

Peggy Lee was a beauty, a smart lady who, as they say, never forgot where she was from.

She was born in Jamestown, N.D., seventh of eight children. She lived briefly in Hillsboro, Fargo, Valley City, and other towns, and she sang "gigs" all over North Dakota. She and her family were Lutherans. Her father, who left home in her teens, was Swedish-American and her mother, who died when she was four, was Norwegian-American.

"Her story is one of sheer survival and enormous talent," says radio man George Brooks, who knew her from her early days. She first sang on station KOVC in Valley City. Ken Kennedy, of Fargo station WDAY, changed her name from Norma Egstrom to Peggy Lee, and she headed for Los Angeles at age 17. Not many young girls at 17 would leave home to try to get into show business. She was a singer, songwriter, actress and composer. One of her hottest hits was *Fever*. She was nominated for 12 Grammy Awards, winning one for her 1969 hit *Is That All There Is?* She was active in her career from 1941 to 2000.

She loved men and they loved her. She was married four times. All ended in divorce. She never forgot North Dakotans and many tell stories about how she would invite them backstage. If you ever met Peggy Lee, you would remember how beautiful she was and her friendly, North Dakota hug.

*Lawrence **Welk*** was the kind of man who kept running until he got there.

He was born in the German-speaking community of Strasburg, N.D., and was the sixth of eight children. His biographer says his family spent their first cold North Dakota winter inside an upturned wagon covered with sod. Welk left the fourth grade to go to work full time on the family farm. At age 21 he decided to go into a music career.

But to play in his early North Dakota days meant driving with his band over snow covered, icy roads, sometimes for 100 miles, to a gig. Five of them slept and changed clothes in their car because they could not afford hotel rooms. His band started to play "light and bubbly champagne music," which the people liked. It was not an easy life. He had to drive over the icy and poor roads in order to book engagements in bars and small night clubs. But he did not give up.

He was married for 61 years and had three children. The Lawrence Welk Show was conservative. He played show tunes, polkas and novelty songs. He would often leave his bandstand and dance with a pretty girl. The audience loved it. He once fired a singer because she showed too much of her leg. He didn't want too much "cheese cake" on his show. Some people thought his music was corny. Others didn't like his "ah-one and ah-two" and his accent ("Wunnerful, Wunnerful"). This did not bother Welk, as he laughed the whole way to the bank.

Growing up in North Dakota, ***Eric Sevareid*** said, "I would not change my boyhood for any man."

Eric Sevareid was born in 1932 in Velva, N.D. His family moved to Minot, N.D., after a bank failure. He graduated from the University of Minnesota, and once he and a friend canoed from Minneapolis to the Hudson Bay.

He joined CBS as a radio announcer but he was moved to television because of his good looks. As a war correspondent, he covered many of the major battles of World War II. Flying over Burma one day, he had to parachute out of a disabled airplane. He always said he grabbed a bottle of gin for the trip down. He often watched from his rooftop as German planes dropped their bombs on London.

He wrote five books and spoke six languages.

He married Lois Finger, Belén Marshall and Suzanne St. Pierre, and had three children. I once worked on a public relations project with Sevareid and I was impressed by his calm, thoughtful manner. With a smile, he said his Scandinavian heritage caused people to think he was "stuffy." He said, "I am all mush inside."

Fargo has not forgotten **Roger Maris**. And they never will.

He attended Fargo High School and transferred to Shanley High School where one day he returned four kicks (two kickoffs, one punt, one interception) for touchdowns.

He met his wife Patricia in the tenth grade when both of them were attending a basketball game. Roger played American Legion baseball in Fargo and in 1952 he played for the Fargo-Moorhead Twins of the Northern League.

He played 11 seasons in the major leagues. He hit 61 home runs in 1961—making him a national celebrity. He beat Babe Ruth's record of 60 home runs—and the Babe Ruth fans never forgave him!

Maris, who batted left and threw right handed, played on four major league teams: Cleveland Indians, Kansas City Athletics, New York Yankees, and St. Louis Cardinals. Aside from being a heavy hitter, he was also respected for his defense play.

In his first game for the Yankees he hit a single, a double and two home runs. The Yankee owners were very pleased!!! Maris was never popular with the sports writers and he never wasted time by trying to win their love. He just concentrated on hitting the ball—and he hit it often.

Maris won many honors which included the North Dakota Rough Riders Award. Other tributes include the Roger Maris Museum at the West Acres Fargo Shopping Center and the Roger Maris Cancer Center at Sanford Hospital in Fargo.

Maris was diagnosed with Non-Hodgkin lymphoma in 1983 and he died of the disease at the age of 51. He is buried at Holy Cross Cemetery in Fargo.

She was born Angeline Brown in Kulm, N.D., in 1931. She became **Angie Dickinson** in 1952, when she married Gene Dickinson, a football player. She kept her married name after their divorce.

Her father, a newspaperman, was also the projectionist at the local movie theater. So she fell in love with the movies at an early age.

When she was 10, her family moved to California. In the early 1950's, while working as a secretary, she entered a beauty contest and placed second. The exposure brought her to the attention of a television producer, who asked her to consider a career in acting. She studied the craft and a few years later was approached by NBC to guest-star on a number of variety shows. While keeping her secretarial job, she worked on Jimmy Durante's tv show and took acting classes four nights a week. "I knew it was a rough business to get into," Dickinson said. But she never gave up.

She soon met Frank Sinatra, becoming a lifelong friend and an associate of his "Rat Pack," along with Dean Martin, Sammy Davis, Jr., Peter Lawford, Joey Bishop, and Shirley MacLaine.

Dickinson's first big movie was the 1959 western classic, *Rio Bravo*, with John Wayne and Dean Martin. In her six decade career, she has appeared in more than 50 films, including the first *Ocean's 11*.

Perhaps her biggest success was *Police Woman*, in which she proved that a female lead could carry an hour-long tv series, and for which she earned a Golden Globe award and Emmy nominations as L.A. police officer Sgt. Pepper Anderson. In 1987, the Los Angeles Police Department awarded her an honorary doctorate. She said, "Now you can call me Doctor Pepper."

Born in 1858, **Theodore Roosevelt** was a sickly child with debilitating asthma, but he overcame his physical health problems by embracing a strenuous lifestyle.

In 1883, when he was 24 years old, he arrived in the badlands of North Dakota to kill a buffalo. He built a ranch named Elkhorn, which was 35 miles north of Medora, N.D. He learned to ride western style, rope and hunt on the banks of the Little Missouri. At the Elkhorn Ranch he grieved for his first wife and mother who both had died on St. Valentine's Day 1884. He ranched and hunted there until 1887.

He became Vice President of the United States in 1901. He became President later that year following the assassination of President William McKinley.

Throughout his life, he maintained a deep love for this state. As the greatest conservationist ever to occupy the White House, he worked hard to preserve North Dakota, leaving his mark in the state with a National Game Preserve, two National Wildlife Refuges, a federal irrigation project and a National Forest.

Although he was born in New York City, North Dakotans regard him as one of our own. He said, "I never would have been President of the United States if it had not been for my experiences in North Dakota."

All of the people in this chapter achieved great success in highly competitive fields because they never gave up!

*About the Author**

Lawrence "Larry" Aasen was born on December 5, 1922, in a log house on a farm near Gardner, North Dakota in very bad snow storm. The doctor could not get there but Aasen was born. North Dakotans never give up.

Aasen graduated from Hillsboro High School in 1941. He attended North Dakota State University 1941-43, and graduated from the University of North Dakota in 1947. He received a Masters' Degree in Public Relations from Boston University in 1949 after serving in the glider section of the 13th Airborne Division in France during World War II. For 38 years he worked in New York City. He served a number of years as a vice president for New York Life Insurance Company as well as in other capacities in journalism and public relations.

*I am not as pretty as I used to be.

He wrote this book because he wanted to honor those North Dakota pioneers who came to North Dakota and stayed. They started farms, towns, churches, schools — and took on the Depression, crop failures, snow storms and loneliness. They did not give up.

Aasen has written four books on North Dakota and many articles. He and his wife from Mississippi live in Westport, Connecticut.